D1707498

The Crown of Ireland

Breandán Ó Buachalla's *The Crown of Ireland* is the third in an occasional series of research papers commissioned by the Centre for Irish Studies at the National University of Ireland, Galway. The series is designed to bring innovative research in Irish Studies to as broad an audience as possible, and to provide a model for the future development of the discipline.

The Centre for Irish Studies was established at NUI, Galway in 2000 and is dedicated to research and advanced teaching on the cultural, social, and political endeavours of Irish people on the island of Ireland and beyond.

Details of the Centre's programmes in teaching and research are available at http://www.nuigalway.ie /centre_irish_ studies/

Other titles in this series:

Joep Leerssen
Hidden Ireland, Public Sphere
(Arlen House, 2002)

Luke Gibbons
Gaelic Gothic: Race, Colonization and Irish Culture
(Arlen House, 2004)

The Crown of Ireland

Breandán Ó Buachalla

ARLEN
HOUSE

The moral rights of the author have been asserted.

ISBN 10: 1–903631–41–6
ISBN 13: 978–1–903631–41–6

First published in October 2006 by Arlen House

Arlen House
PO Box 222
Galway
Phone/Fax: 00 353 86 8207617
Email: arlenhouse@gmail.com

Distributed in North America by Syracuse University Press

Syracuse University Press
621 Skytop Road, Suite 110
Syracuse, NY 13244–5290
Phone: 315–443–5534/Fax: 315–443–5545
Email: supress@syr.edu

Editorial: Centre for Irish Studies, NUI, Galway
Cover image: Seán Mannion
Typesetting: Arlen House
Printed in Ireland

Bord na
Leabhar
Gaeilge

CONTENTS

ACKNOWLEDGEMENTS

An early version of this essay was read at post-graduate seminars in the Department of Celtic Languages and Literatures, Harvard University (October 2001) and the Keough Institute for Irish Studies, University of Notre Dame (April 2002). I would like to thank those who attended the seminars and, in particular, those who contributed to the discussion. I would also like to thank Dr Louis de Paor for helpful comments and suggestions. Naturally, I alone am responsible for the presentation and interpretation of the material.

The front cover image is reproduced by permission of the Folger Shakespeare Library.

Thanks are also due to the following:
National Library of Ireland
The National Museum of Ireland
The British Library
Trinity College Dublin
Royal Irish Academy
Armagh Public Library
Dublin Public Library

ILLUSTRATIONS

Fig. 1: The 'crowned harp' as found in a charter of Queen Elizabeth to the city of Dublin 1583. Source: J.T. Gilbert, *Facsimiles of National manuscripts of Ireland* IV/1, London, 1882 (frontispiece).

Fig. 2: Drawing of Noah in the Book of Ballymote (*c.* 1400, RIA). Source: Hayes-McCoy (1979: 133).

Fig. 3: Wall fresco in Knockmoy Abbey, Co. Roscommon. Source: Hayes-McCoy (1979: 133).

Fig. 4: Cartoon of 'Uncrowned Monarch'. Source: National Library.

Fig. 5: Portrait of Brian Bóramha 'Monarch of Ireland'. Source: O'Connor (1723, frontispiece).

Fig. 6: Map and emblem of Ireland in Diego Homem's atlas (1558). Source: British Library.

Fig. 7: O'Connell's 'Repeal Cap'. Source: National Museum.

Fig. 8: Cover of *O'Connell Centenary Record 1875* (Dublin, 1878).

The Crown of Ireland

Fig. 1: Crowned Harp as found in a charter of
Queen Elizabeth to the city of Dublin 1583

The writing of history in early modern Europe took, for the
most part, two forms: the traditional chronicle in the
medieval annalistic mode and the new mode of continuous
narrative as practiced by humanist historians. Bouchart's
Les grandes croniques de Bretagne, Gilles's *Les chroniques et
annales de France*, Stow's *Annals of England*, and The Four
Masters' *Annála Ríoghachta Éireann* are typical examples of
the former; Guicciardini's *La Historia d'Italia*, de Mariana's
Historia general de España, Du Haillan's *Histoire de France*,
and Séathrún Céitinn's *Foras Feasa ar Éirinn* exemplify the
latter. The contrast can be overdrawn, of course, since the
disparate genres were sometimes blurred as chronicles
grew from one-line entries to connected prose, as they
expanded from local to national horizons, and as they
moved from ancient to modern events.[1] Nevertheless, if
Momigliano's (1950: 286) assertion that 'the whole modern
method of historical research is founded upon the

distinction between original and derivative authorities' is valid, then the origins of modern historiography can, undoubtedly, be located in Renaissance humanism.[2]

The Renaissance humanists were the first to make a concerted effort to study the past with some appreciation of temporal perspective. When the French scholar La Popelinière (1599) initiated his project for writing a 'histoire nouvelle des François', it was obvious to him and his scholarly colleagues that a new kind of history was in the making, one which was to be differentiated from both medieval chronicles and ancient histories alike. And although the notion that the departure entailed an 'historiographical revolution' (Fussner 1962) has been questioned, it is a given that a new historical awareness had arisen, one which emphasised the necessity of using primary sources and which saw its function as constructing a 'perfect history' (*histoire accomplie/historia integra/historia perfecta*). In particular this meant including ecclesiastical as well as civic and military affairs; in general terms it entailed a review of the entire heritage: a method, not only for reconstructing the past, but also for making sense of it. The value of history was no longer either moral or private, but public and political; its importance related, now, not to the past but to the present and the future. The real originality of La Popelienière's work, however, was in effect to historicize the discipline of history, to devise a stadial scheme 'to describe the trajectories of national historiographies' (Kelley 1998: 195).

If the new historicism in general was the product of Renaissance humanism, the specific forms and interpretations of history it generated were shaped, in particular, by the upheavals of the Reformation and by national rivalries. And although partisanship often distorted historical perspective, yet the rhetoric of historical impartiality, disinterested curiosity and scientific aspirations remained. As a consequence, new perspectives on church history coloured by confessional allegiance, and new perspectives on political history coloured by nationalism, sought to reshape the medieval past. Religious rivalry, the burgeoning of the notion of *patria*, national consciousness, the cultivation throughout Europe of the humanistic national history as initiated by Polydorus Virgil, all reinforced what Dumoulin taught: only the nation could now be 'an intelligible field of study' (Kelley 1970: 181). Historians, all over Europe, were creating what Helgerson (1992: 22) has called, with reference to England, a 'rhetoric of nationhood'. They also established the authority of historical criticism.

Séathrún Céitinn (*c*. 1580–1644), was the first to provide a national narrative in a modern idiom for Ireland. Born near Cahir, in Co. Tipperary, he seems to have attended a school of traditional learning in his youth and to have been ordained in Ireland before leaving in 1603 for further education in Bordeaux and Rheims. He was back in Ireland and engaged in parochial duties in his native county by 1613. Like many of his learned colleagues who had been trained abroad, he was both poet and priest, preacher and prose-writer, theologian and historian. In Ireland, perhaps more than anywhere else in Europe, the Renaissance and the Reformation were from the beginning completely intertwined and the great flowering of Irish prose which occurred in the seventeenth century owed its dynamic ultimately to the confluence of those two movements. Céitinn's *oeuvre* reflects that confluence both in its subject-matter and its underlying ideology. His major theological works – *Eochairsciath an Aifrinn* (a tract on the mass) and *Trí Biorghaoithe an Bháis* (a tract on death) – were written primarily for the clergy who were thereby provided with some of the necessary polemical and pastoral tools for their mission. His historiographical work – *Foras Feasa ur Éirinn* ('the basis of knowledge on Ireland') – was intended for a far wider audience.

Foras Feasa ar Éirinn was begun in the 1620s, it would seem, and was completed about 1634. The main text comprises two books. The first deals with the history of Ireland from the beginning of time to the coming of Christianity; the second continues the narrative from the fifth century down to the coming of the Normans in the twelfth. Appended to the main text is a collection of genealogies and tables of synchronisms. But although the narrative formally ends with Gabháltas Gall ('The Invasion of the Foreigners') in the twelfth century, its encoding framework and its trenchant foreword are firmly focused on contemporaneous politico-religious issues. Céitinn's immediate purpose in writing FFÉ, was to refute the 'falsehoods' concerning Ireland and her inhabitants which were being propagated in the writings of the twelfth-century Giraldus Cambrensis and in the works of the contemporary writers Camden, Stanihurst, Spenser, Davies and others. It is highly significant that, in demolishing their malicious falsehoods, Céitinn applied to them contemporary historiographical criteria. As regards Cambrensis, there was not 'a lay nor a letter, old record nor ancient text, chronicle nor annals' which could support his lie (FFÉ i: 18); Campion was more like a player on a platform recounting derisive stories than a historian (FFÉ i: 62); Moryson's work could not be afforded "the dignity of history" since he had ignored the rules appropriate to the writing of history as laid down by Polydorus Vergil (FFÉ i: 56); those writers were but retelling 'tales of false witnesses' (FFÉ i: 76) who were hostile to Ireland and ignorant of her history; they, unlike him, had not access to the primary sources and, even if they had, they could not understand them, since they were ignorant of the language in which they were written: *Do chonnairc mé agus tuigim prímhleabhbair an tseanchusa, agus ní fhacadarsan iad, agus dá bhfaicdís ní tuigfidhe leo iad.* (FFÉ i: 76).

Céitinn, it is obvious, had absorbed the new historical awareness and was manifestly conversant with current historiography, but in replacing the falsehoods of foreign writers with his own retelling of Irish history, he was addressing himself not to the past but to contemporaneous issues. The story of Ireland, as presented in *Foras Feasa ar Éirinn* provided a common historical heritage for both Gael and Sean-Ghall who henceforth were to be subsumed under the common denomination of *Éireannaigh* and whose identity was characterized by valour, learning and their steadfastness 'in the Catholic faith' (FFÉ i: 78). It also provided historical legitimisation for current political attitudes among the socio-cutlural elites of early Stuart Ireland. In particular it provided the necessary historical validation for the acceptance of Charles I (1625–49) 'our present king' (FFÉ i: 208), whose legitimacy, and that of his father James I (1603–25), could be confirmed by the traditional validatory mechanisms of prophecy (FFÉ i: 206) and genealogy (FFÉ ii: 386). To the received canon of traditional lore Céitinn had grafted, in a most sophisticated manner, a contemporaneous perspective which took cognizance of, and was a reponse to, the political realities of his own day. He had also produced a work of major literary achievement. Not only did he successfully assimilate in one continuous narrative the various strata and components of traditional lore (mythology, hagiography, genealogy, folklore, chronology), but he masterfully recast that narrative in an intelligible modern idiom. For Céitinn's primary aim of ensuring that the history of Ireland and her people did not go unrecorded, was executed with an unprecedented and unsurpassed felicity of language and style. Within twenty years of its composition it had been subsumed into the living literary tradition and it continued to function therein, as a veritable *foras feasa*, until the second half of the nineteenth century.

Historians' understanding and interpretation of seventeenth-century Irish historiography have undergone a profound mutation in recent years. Changing attitudes to *Foras Feasa ar Éirinn* constitute a case in point. As late as 1988 Foster (1988: 43), quoting Dunne, characterized Céitinn's seminal work as 'a monument to a doomed civilization'. It is a measure of the historiographical revolution that has since taken place that in the most recent and comprehensive study of the text (Cunningham 2000), Foster's characterization is not even mentioned, let alone discussed; his derivative interpretation is now *passé* it seems. In the meantime the revisionary approach to *Foras Feasa ar Éirinn* has come to be generally accepted. According to that interpretation, *Foras Feasa ar Éirinn* is to be seen as an Irish analogue to the national humanistic history then in vogue in Europe. Far from it being an exercise in antiquarianism or in retrospective obituary it was written very much with an eye to the present and the future. Céitinn's perspective on the past, like that of his European colleagues, was dictated by the exigencies of the present.[3] Indeed, both *Foras Feasa ar Éirinn* and its companion volume *Annála Ríoghachta Éireann* provide apposite Irish realizations of the general dictum that:

> Though it must be stated with the greatest possible caution, it would seem that the place of history in early-modern cultures was that of 'legitimator' and 'codifier' of the internal and international institutional changes which occurred. History only rarely inspired new definitions of national consciousness and political power, but it did coherently depict recent institutional and intellectual shifts by changing the 'canon' of accepted truths about the national past to reflect new political realities.
>
> (Ranun 1975:11)

Another example is provided by the historiographical work known today as *The Annals of Clonmacnoise* (AC).[4]

This text which was originally entitled, it seems, 'a history of the kings of Ireland' has come down to us only in translation. It was written in 1627 by the Irish scholar Conall Mag Eochagáin (Conell Mageoghan) of Lismoyney, Co. Westmeath for his friend and kinsman Toirdhealbhach Mag Cochláin (Torlogh Mac Coghlan) Lord of Delvin. In the course of the work, Mageoghan regularly quotes Irish phrases and poems and he refers several times to the Irish original:

> The earnest desire I understand you have to know these things made me undertake the translatinge of the old Irish booke for you which by long lying shutt and unused I could hardly read ...
>
> (A: ii, AC: 9)[5]

> The old Irish book out of which I writ this is soe overtorne and rent that the characters of the very letters are quite lost in some places, soo as I must be content to translate what I can reade ...
>
> (A: 14r, AC: 52)

> There are soe manie leaves lost or stolen out of the old Irish booke which I translate, that I doe nott know how to handle itt; Butt to satisfye your request, I will translate such places in the booke as I can read ... for I goe by the woords of the old booke and not by my owne invention, which is soe illfavouredly and confusedly handled, that myne author could not get his penn to name the kinges of England or other forraine countryes by their proper names but by such Irish names as he pleased to devise out of his owne head, although he was a greate Latinist and Scholler ...
>
> (A: 64r, AC: 215)

He does not, however, name either 'myne author' or the scribe of his exemplar, nor has the original text ever been located or identified.[6] Mageoghan's autograph copy of his translation is now also lost but several derivatives of it survive, the earliest copies being dated to 1660 and 1661 respectively.

In format and style *The Annals of Clonmacnoise* corresponds to other annalistic compilations and its subject-matter parallels similar material emanating from what has been called 'the Clonmacnoise group' of annals.[7] Accordingly, in spite of the absence of primary corroborative evidence, scholars have generally accepted Mageoghan's work as genuine. It was, according to Paul Walsh (1932: 81), 'a very fine and very valuable translation,' while O'Curry (1861:130) claimed that the translator 'well understood the value of the original Gaedhlic phraseology, and rendered it every justice, as far as we can determine in the absence of the original'. John O'Donovan (1861: xlii) was more cautious and, it seems, more perceptive: the translation was, he claimed, 'a work which professed to be a faithful version of the original, although in some instances it has obviously been interpolated by the translator'. Binchy (1961: 67) perceived it to be more of 'a paraphrase' rather than a translation. In one significant feature *The Annals of Clonmacnoise* seems to be unique in Irish annalistic material. A central leitmotif running through the compilation, from the pre-Patrician period down to the twelfth century, is the notion of 'the Crown of Ireland':

(a) Betweene which 4 houses the Crowne of Ireland ranne for the most parte in diebus illis untill the conquest of Ireland by Kinge Henry the 2nd, kinge of England.

(A: 11v, AC: 43)

(b) The 3 chiefe houses in Ireland were ... the house of Cashell in Munster, the house of Crwagha in Connaght and of Eawyn Macha in Ulster; Betweene which three houses the Crowne of Ireland rested a great while.

(A: 12r, AC: 46)

(c) When Kinge Twahall was thus established in the quite possession of the Crowne and Kingdome and had brought the whole Kingdome into his subjection ... the Kinge ... enjoyned all the nobility ... that none of them nor annie of them would make claime to the Crowne ... and that they should suffour him and his heires and successors quietly to enjoy the Crowne for ever.

(A: 14r, AC: 52)

(d) Butt the Saint ... cursed the Kinge and his posterity for ever, and humbly besought God of his infinite power that none of that Kings posterity should ever after inherite the Crowne of Ireland.

(A: 18v, AC: 68)

(e) This is the church of that clarke that prophesied that none of my fathers posterity should inherite that Crowne of Ireland.

(A: 20r, AC: 74)

(f) K. Moylseaghlin of his greate bounty and favour to learninge and learned men bestowed the revenewes of the Crowne of Ireland for one yeare upon McCoissy.

(A: 46v, AC: 161)

(g) Donnogh mac Bryen Borow was kinge as some saye, and was soone deposed again, and went to Rome to doe pennance ... he brought the Crowne of Ireland with him thither, which remayned with the Popes untill Pope Adrian gave the same to Kinge Henry the second that conquered Ireland.

(A: 51v, AC: 179)

A comparison with corresponding passages in other annalistic and historiographical material, where the same events and/or personages are recorded, is revealing. As regards Tuathal Techtmhar (item *c*), The Annals of Tigearnach merely record his reign: *Tuathal Techtmhar regnavit annis xxx* (RC 16: 419); while the regnal material in

'Do Fhlathiusaib hÉrend' records that the 'kingship' was promised to his family forever: *ríge dia chlaindseom co bráth* (LL: 23b 30). In several poems in which reference is made to Mac Coisi (item *f*) it is stated that what Maoil Sheachlainn bestowed on him was *ceannas Éireann* ('the governance of Ireland'):

Éirigh go Teamhraigh na dtréad,
mar a tá mo shealbhadh séad:
caith bliadhain ón oidhche a-nocht
i gceannas Éireann na n-ardphort.

Go to Tara of the flocks,
where my possession of treasures is;
spend a year from to-night
in the governance of Ireland of the high strongholds.

(Bergin 1921: 177 § 9)[8]

Fuaras ní budh mó iná soin:
ceannas Éireann toir is tiar
feadh bliadhna ó fhlaith Locha Laoi …
mé Mac Coissi ceann na gcliar.

I received something greater than that:
the governance of Ireland east and west
for a year from the lord of Loch Laoi …
I am Mac Coissi the head of the poets.

(Meyer 1907: 305 §§ 5, 8)

As regards Donnchadh mac Briain (item *g*), the major annalistic and historical compilations are at one in recording his pilgrimage to Rome and his death there:

Donnchadh mac Briain Boroma, rí Muman, do athrighadh & a dul do Roim dia ailithri, co n-erbuilt iar mbuaidh n-aithrighe a mainistir Sdefain.

Donnchadh, son of Brian Boroma, king of Munster, was dethroned, and went to Rome on a pilgrimage, and there died, in the monastery of Stephen, after victory of repentance.

(RC 17: 400)

Donnchadh mac Briain, airdrí Mumhan, do aithríoghadh, [7] a dhul do Róimh iarsin, co n-erbailt fo bhuaidh aithrighe i mainistir Stephain mairtír.

Donnchadh, son of Brian, chief king of Munster, was deposed; and he afterwards went to Rome, where he died, under the victory of penance, in the monastery of Stephan the martyr.

(ARÉ ii: 886)

Dá éis sin do cuireadh Donnchadh mac Briain a ríoghacht agus do chuaidh da oilithre don Róimh go bhfuair bás ann i mainistir Steapháin.

After this Donnchadh, son of Brian, was deposed from his kingship, and went on a pilgrimage to Rome, where he died in the monastery of St. Stephen.

(FFÉ iii: 292)

Nowhere in these excerpts, nor in parallel passages in other compilations, is there any reference to Mageoghan's ubiquitous term 'the crown of Ireland'. That is not surprising, given that for the period in question (ancient, early and medieval Ireland) neither the concept nor the term is attested; no Irish equivalent existed. It could be argued that perhaps Mageoghan had substituted his term for an original authentic one like *ríghe Éireann* 'the kingship of Ireland' or *ceannas Éireann* 'the governance of Ireland', since the term is used by him both as an abstract noun and metonymically. Nevertheless, it is also obvious from excerpt (g) above, and other examples in the text, that the term also denotes a concrete artefact which Donnchadh, the son of Brian Bóramha, took with him to Rome.

Fig. 2: Drawing of Noah in the Book of Ballymote

Fig. 3: Wall fresco in Knockmoy Abbey, Co. Roscommon

The notion of a 'king of Ireland' (*rí Éireann*) is, of course, an ancient one and is a central and common concept in Irish literature and Irish politics, from the seventh century to the nineteenth. When Domnall mac Aeda died in AD 641, the Annals of Ulster record the event as *Mors Domnaill m. Aedo regis Hibernie* (Mac Airt 1983: 122); when in 1828 Daniel O'Connell, the first popular leader of Catholic Ireland, was elected as MP for county Clare, he assumed the mantle of 'the uncrowned king of Ireland'. Irish kings were never crowned, however, nor was an artefact such as a crown ever associated with their regal ordination. In the traditional accounts of the inauguration of Irish kings that have come down to us, the cultural artefacts utilised in the ceremony were a wand and a single shoe:

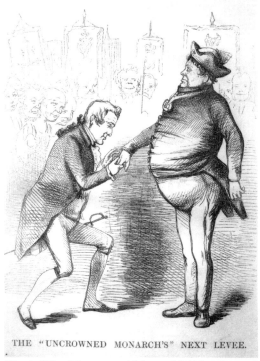

THE "UNCROWNED MONARCH'S" NEXT LEVEE.

Fig. 4: "The 'Uncrowned Monarch's' Next Levee"

It was the hereditary privilege of the O'Maolconry to be alone on the sacred mound of Carn Fraoich, with the newly inaugurated King, whom he presented to the assembled chieftains of the Province, and recited the royal genealogy. He then administered the oath to observe the customs of Conaught, placed the gift shoe on the King's foot as a pledge of homage and submission on the part of the chieftains and put into his hand the white wand or scepter, the emblem of sovereignty, and finally recorded the proceedings.

(Curtis 1941: 131)[9]

There is some pictorial evidence and, perhaps, some archaeological evidence for the existence of crowns/ diadems in medieval Ireland. There are also, of course, numerous references in Irish literature to kings and other socially important personages wearing a crown, a diadem or a tiara, but they are always described, it seems, as part of the apparel only; they never have any symbolic or ideological import.[10] It is only towards the end of the sixteenth century that the crown, for the first time ever, assumes symbolic signification and function in the ideology of Irish kingship. The context in which it arose was, undoubtedly, what Bradshaw (1979) has called 'the Irish constitutional revolution': the act of 1541 which declared Henry VIII to be king of Ireland and which changed the constitutional status of Ireland from a Lordship to a Kingdom.

According to medieval theory, Ireland was the feudal property of the Holy See which had been entrusted by papal grant to the lordship of the English monarch. In 1540 Henry VIII was advised by his Irish council to bring in an act 'that the King and his successors be Kings of Ireland'. Such an act was necessary, it was claimed, since it was generally believed in Ireland that the 'regal estate' of the island rested in the papacy and that the lordship enjoyed by the kings of England was 'but a governance under the obedience of the same'; furthermore it was also obvious that the inhabitants of the realm of Ireland 'have not been so obedient to the King's highness as they ought to have been' (Curtis 1943: 77).The primary motive, then, of the act of 1541 was to copper-fasten the legal claim of the crown to Ireland and to bring within its dominion – for the first time – all the inhabitants of Ireland, irrespective of their cultural or ethnic background. In establishing Ireland as a distinct kingdom, with its own king – the king of Ireland – the act did, in theory at least, establish parity between the two kingdoms. It also provided a constitutional framework within which notions of autonomy could develop and it established the legal and constitutional existence of 'the crown of this realm of Ireland'.[11] The concept of the 'crown of Ireland' was not only a legal or constitutional entity; it also had political implications, as was recognized by no less a personage than Sir George Carew. In 'A Discourse of Ireland' which he forwarded to Sir Richard Cecil, 'her Majesty's principal secretary', in 1601, Carew contrasts the aims of the English and the Irish thus:

> The English race and the Irish have different endes: the English to recover againe, the supreme government in bearinge her Majesty's sworde by one of themselves, as for many years and adges they have done … The Irish Lords ayme at a higher marke, still retayninge in memory that theire ancestors have been monarckes, and provyncial kings of this land, and therefore to recover theire former greatness, they kicke at the government, and enter into rebellion, losing no tyme of advantage or refusinge the least forrayne ayde, that may (by troublinge the State) advance their desires, hoping in tyme (by stronge hands) to regaine the Crowne of Ireland to themselves.
> (Brewer 1870: 168)[12]

One result of the politico-religious wars of the sixteenth century was the recognition of the geographical importance of Ireland. 'He that will England win/through Ireland must come in', ran the contemporary prophecy, a sentiment which both reflected and influenced contemporary strategies on both sides. The numerous appeals for military aid which were made by Irish leaders, both civil and religious, to Spain, France and the Papacy in the second half of the sixteenth century were all predicated on a simple *quid pro quo*: in return for military aid the foreign power would be granted the 'crown of Ireland'.[13] Thus, O Neill and O Donnell in their correspondence with the Spanish court always stressed the political prize available to the succourer of the Irish:

> If the king of Spain will send them timely aid he will restore to them religion, and for himself acquire a Kingdom … Ireland will acknowledge no other king than his Catholic Majesty.
>
> (CSPI 1592–6: 407–9)

It was reported in 1551 that a group of Irishmen were engaged in sustained efforts at the French court to induce the King, Henri II, 'to accept the crown of Ireland and to annex it to his Scottish kingdom' (Lyons 2003: 100). In 1559 one Alexander Lynch, acting as an agent for a confederacy of bishops and temporal lords, offered the throne of Ireland to a king of Philip II's choice; in return they sought a Spanish force to be sent to free Ireland from English rule (Silke 1966: 5). In a letter of 1569 addressed by the 'Bishops and Nobles of Ireland' to 'his Holiness and his Catholic Majesty' they inform Philip II that:

> Accordingly they have decided, with the help of God and the favour of the most clement Catholic King, to accept the person of any Catholic and valiant Prince from his Catholic Majesty's kin, whether of the house of Spain or Burgundy, whom his catholic majesty may nominate; and to receive, recognise and crown him as their true, legitimate and

natural king, thereby restoring the royal throne of this island, and to revere the presence of one king, one faith, and one kingdom.

(Binchy 1921: 366)

However novel that strategy, and its attendant rhetoric, may be judged in the light of the historical record, it was presented by those involved not as a new departure, but rather as a return to a former state, a process of 'restoring the royal throne of this island'. Moreover it is implicit in it and in similar statements that, in spite of the act of 1541, Irish nobles and clerics were acting as if the crown was theirs to bestow. A similar conceit pervades several poems written in Irish around the same time, though in these sources the crown is being claimed, not for foreign princes, but for the native lords. In a poem to Cú Chonnacht Mag Uidhir (†1589), Lord of Fermanagh, the poet Fearghal Óg Mac an Bhaird complains that, since Donnchadh, the son of Brian Bóramha, took the crown of Ireland with him to Rome, there had been no 'crowned chief' (*triath corónta*) in Ireland; as a result, Ireland was now the only country in Europe without a 'highking' (*gan airdrígh*):

Cia re bhfuil Éire ag anmhain?
mó is righin dá ríoghdhamhnaibh ...

Créad an corsa ar Inis Ír?
ní fhuil oiléan gan airdrígh
feadh seinEorpa ó mhuir go muir
acht bean cheineolta Chobhthaigh.

Fágbhais Banbha bean Logha
Donnchadh mac Briain Bhóramha;
scéal dob fhairbríogh le Fiadh Fáil
triall an airdríogh don Eadáil.

Coróin ríoghachta fear bhFáil
rug leis a hÉirinn fhódbháin ...

In Éirinn na n-eas dtana
ní raibhe i ndiaidh Dhonnchadha
– ní tuar onóra d'Iath Bhreagh –
triath corónta[14] dár creideadh.

For whom is Ireland waiting? heirs - apparent are slow to
appear ...

What is the plight of Ireland? There is no island without a
highking throughout old Europe from sea to sea except the
rightful wife of Cobhthach (.i. Ireland).

Donnchadh son of Brian Bóramha left Banbha the wife of
Lugh; it was a burden to Ireland that the highking should
journey to Italy.

He brought the crown of the kingdom of Ireland with him
from Ireland of the fair sod ...

In Ireland of the shallow streams there was not a crowned
chief who was given allegiance after Donnchadh – it is not an
omen of honour for Ireland.

(Greene 1972: ii §§1, 2, 4, 5, 6)

In a eulogy on Conn Ó Néill (†1559), the story of the
crown being brought to Rome is again recounted and Ó
Néill's claim to it extolled and established.[15] In these and
other poems from the same period we come, for the first
time, on the epithets triath/flaith/rí corónta ('crowned
lord/prince/king') being applied to the native leaders.

In an elegy on Aodh Ruadh Ó Domhnaill (†1602), his
tragic death in Spain is compared by Fearghal Óg Mac an
Bhaird to the equally diasastrous death of Brian Bóramha
'the crowned prince of the Irish race' (flaith chorónta Chraoi
na bhFionn); in the series of poems known as Iomarbhágh na
bhFileadh, one of the questions discussed is the legitimacy of
the means by which Brian 'the crowned king of Ireland'
(rígh corónta ar Éirinn) assumed the kingship; in one poem it

is claimed that any king after Maoil Sheachlainn (†1022) who assumed the sovereignty of Ireland was not 'a crowned highking' (*níor bha hairdrí corónta*):

> Mac Cinnéidigh, cian ó shoin,
> tug Brian a bhás 's a bheathaidh,
> flaith chorónta Chraoi na bhFionn,
> ar aoi onóra Éireann.

Brian Mac Cinnéidigh, the crowned prince of the Irish, long ago gave his life and death for the honour of Ireland.

(Breatnach 1973: 45 §57)

> Acht do Bhrian Bóraimhe amháin,
> ní raibh iar gcreideamh d'Íbh Táil,
> iná fós d'fhuil Éibhir Fhinn,
> 'na rígh corónta ar Éirinn.

Except for Brian Bóraimhe alone, there was no one of Í Tháil nor even of the blood of Éibhear Fionn who was a crowned king of Ireland.

(Mhág Craith 1967: 38 § 64)

> Aoinfhear d'uaislibh chríche Coinn
> iarsan bhfíorfhlaith Maoil Sheachlainn
> dar fhaoi le flaitheas bhFódla,
> níor bha hairdrí corónta …

Not one of the nobles of Ireland, after the rightful ruler Maoil Sheachlainn, who married the sovereignty of Fódla, was a crowned high-king.

(ibid. 39 §100)[16]

> Dá leanadh Brian, mar mhaoidhe,
> lorg canóine gan chlaoine,
> aithríoghadh dob olc an bhreath
> ar rígh chorónta chráibhtheach.

Had Brian, as you claim, honestly followed precedent, it was
an evil counsel of his to dethrone a pious crowned king.

(McKenna 1918: vi §237)

It is obvious that being deemed to be a *rí corónta* had
become in Irish political discourse the ultimate seal of
legitimacy. The term is applied in later poems to both
Charles II and James II and throughout the seventeenth
century the crown is increasingly envisaged as a symbol of
legitimacy and rightful kingship:

> That Sir Phelim O'Neale was borne with the picture of a
> crowne on his side as a signe that he ought to bee theire King.
>
> (TCD MS 814: 61b)

> Thomas Middlebrooke of Leag-MacCaffry in the Parish of
> Drumully … avers that … he heard the said Cahall boy
> McDermott say that within one fortnight they should have a
> newe Kinge of Ireland Crowned of the O'Neales.
>
> (TCD MS 835: 142)

> Go dtí chum críche díbhse an méid se:
> teacht díbh fé neart tar ais gan bhaoghal,
> is bhur Rí corónta romhaibh 'na léadar.
> is Duke of York mar phosta cléire …

> That this may come to pass for you:
> that you will return in strength without danger,
> and your crowned king [Charles II] leading you,
> and the Duke of York as the prop of the clergy.
>
> (O'Rahilly 1952: v §§ 412–5)

Do bhodhair an tSionainn, an Life, is an Laoi cheolmhar
ó lom an cuireata cluiche ar an rí coróineach.

The Shannon, the Liffey, and the tuneful Lee roared
since the knave [William of Orange] bested the
crowned king [James II] in a game.

(Dinneen 1911: 21 §§ 9–12)

Fig. 5: Portrait of Brian Bóramha 'Monarch of Ireland'

In the course of the century it also became an historical 'fact' that Irish kings had always been crowned and had worn crowns:

Now he [Giraldus Cambrensis] has fallen into a most egregious error, by denying that crowns were ever worn by the Irish kings; whereas our writers state expressly that the diadem which encircled the brows of our Irish kings at their coronation was carried to Rome by Donnchadh, son of Brian Boroimhe ... I read somewhere that Edward Bruce, when proclaimed king of Ireland by the natives received a royal diadem. Which proves that the custom of wearing crowns at their coronation must have been observed by the kings of Ireland.

(Lynch 1662 iii: 327–9)

We read, that the crown was antiently the usual badge of royalty, not only with the provincial kings and queens, but with the supreme kings and monarchs of all Ireland. It is called in the mother tongue *assionn* a word of one syllable, and is said to be made of gold ... R. T. Ward writes, supported by the authority of most of the antiquarians, that all the Kings of Ireland sat crowned with a diadem, as well as in battle, and generally in these solemn and public assemblies. Brian King of Ireland, in the battle of Clontarf, the crown being seen, was immediately known by the enemy, and killed in the year 1014. Historians tell us that the succeeding posterity of him were most solemnly created kings, and decorated with the golden crown. Donnchadh, his son, is reported to have brought with him to Rome the crown of his ancestors, in the year 1064.

(O Flaherty 1685: 68–9)

When a monarch or King was to be inaugurated in Ireland ... one of the chief princes came to him, took his sword from him, and delivered a long, white, unknotty wand or rod into his hand ... Afterwards the Crown (in the Irish language *mionn riogha*, i.e. a royal cap) was put upon his head, which was all made of gold and precious stones ...

(Mac Curtin 1717: 302–3)

> Brian gather'd the power of Leath-Mogha … sent for
> Maoilseachlainn … and spoke to him as followeth … 'I
> wait for your answer, and believe I am come to possess
> and defend the Crown of our great ancestors'.
> Maoilseachluinn after a long silence, thus replied. 'You
> mighty defender of the Irish nation … I shall submit to
> your mercy and yield up my Crown and royal dignity to
> your will' …
>
> (*ibid.* 214–6)

Whatever the basis for the fiction of the Crown of
Ireland being in Rome, it was a widespread belief, it
seems.[17] It was also one which subverted the claims of the
crown of England and was, accordingly, taken seriously. In
1593 Nicholas Whyte of Mayane, Co. Kildare was whipped,
pilloried and imprisoned for

> having traitorously published that there was a prophecy in
> Ireland that O'Donell should be King in Ireland, and that
> there was an old crown of the Kings of Ireland in Rome,
> and that the Catholick Bishops of this land did write to
> Rome for that Crown
>
> (HMC Egmont I: 25).

Mageoghan was not, it is obvious, the originator of the
concept of 'the Crown of Ireland,' nor of the fiction attached
to it; his contribution to its fertile development was his
portrayal of its historical existence – even from pre-
Patrician times. And although his peroration was firmly
grounded in the past (his narrative concludes in the
fifteenth century), it is difficult not to suspect that his
invocation and use of the concept of 'the Crown of Ireland'
related more to contemporaneous political concerns than to
disinterested historical research.

By the end of the sixteenth century the Irish upper
classes had irrevocably aligned themselves to the Church of
Rome; after the battle of Kinsale and particularly after the

Flight of the Earls the over-riding attitude of these classes was one of accommodation. Central to that accommodation was the evolution of a rapprochement with the temporal authority as represented by the King. Under the leadership of Peter Lombard, archbishop of Armagh (1601–25), and applying the theological formula developed by the Jesuit theologians Bellarmine and Suárez, the Irish church taught that James I, albeit an heretical Prince, was nevertheless king of Ireland *de jure* and accordingly was entitled to the allegiance due to Caesar. This was henceforth official Church policy and it is well reflected in the catechismal and spiritual material being provided in Irish by the agents of the Counter-Reformation in Ireland.[18] The intellectual rationalisation and historical legitimation for this new departure were provided by the native intelligentsia who in genealogies, in verse and in prose proclaimed the irrefutable right of the house of Stuart, being themselves in origin Irish, to the kingdom and crown of Ireland.

An early insight into the new attitude is afforded by a poem written, as a prophetic utterance, on James's accession:

Trí coróna i gcairt Shéamais
cia dhíobh nachar dheighfhéaghais? …

Cuirfidhear – is cubhaidh lais –
trí coróna um cheann Shéamais;
ní scéal rúin rádh na leabhar,
gach fádh dhúinn dá dheimhnioghadh.

An chéaduair – cóir a chuimhne –
coróin Alban iathghoirme …

An dara huair – aithnidh dhamh –
cuirfidhear coróin Sagsan …

Prionnsa óg go n-aigneadh ard,
biaidh sise ag Séamas Stíobhard,
onóir nach iomarcach leam,
coróin iongantach Éireann ...

Más cead leis a éisteacht uaim,
sloinnfead a cheart an chéaduair
ar fhionnAlbain na n-iath mín,
triath ionnarbaidh gach eissídh ...

A lámh is díorgha dligheadh –
anois i gcéill cuirfidhear –
ná bí ag teacht ar éineing d'uaim
's do cheart ar Éirinn armruaidh ...

Fada a-tá i dtairngire dhuit
críoch Sagsan – is iúl orrdhruic;
duit is dú Éire amhlaidh,
is tú a céile ar chomhardhaibh. ...

Ní fhuil fuil airdríogh eile
acht fuil meic na maighdine
'ga bhfuil barr uaisleachta ar t'fhuil,
guaisbhearta Gall id ghníomhaibh ...

Three crowns in James's charter – which of them have you
not seen with pleasure ? ...

Three crowns, 'tis fitting for him, shall be placed on James's
head; the utterance of the books is no secret, every seer
confirms it.

First, it is proper to recall, is the crown of black-earthed
Scotland ...

Secondly I know it – the Saxons' crown shall be placed ...

That young prince so high of mind – James Stewart – shall
possess Ireland's wondrous crown; an honour, I know, he
well deserves ...

If he deigns to listen to me, I will first tell of his right
to fair pleasant-fielded Scotland, this lord who banishes all
strife ...

O prince whose hand gives straight judgements, it will now
be said talk not of taking new territory; thou hast already a
right to red-sworded Ireland ...

The Saxons' land – 'tis well known – has been long
prophesied for thee; so likewise is Ireland due to thee;
thou art her spouse by all the signs ...

There is no high-king's blood, however noble save that of the
Virgin's son that surpasses thine ...
(McKenna 1939: 44 §§ 1, 2, 3, 4, 5, 7, 21, 23, 26)

The identification of James as a prince who 'banishes all
strife' (*triath ionnarbaidh gach eissídh*), who dispenses
'straight judgements' (*a lámh as díorgha dligheadh*), who is
deemed to be Ireland's 'spouse' (*is tú a céile ar
chomhardhaibh*) are explicable and meaningful only in the
context of the Irish ideology of kingship. To this
autochtonous ideology the notion of 'the crown of Ireland'
has now been successfully grafted; henceforth that crown
signified the independent authority of the kingdom of
Ireland.

In compiling *Annála Ríoghachta Éireann*[19] the Four
Masters provided, albeit in annalistic mode, a history of
that kingdom from pre-historic times to the year 1616. The
antiquity of that kingdom is also assumed by Séathrún
Céitinn in *Foras Feasa ar Éirinn*; Ireland was 'a kingdom
apart by herself, like a little world' (*do bhí Éire 'na ríoghacht
ar leith léi féin, amhail domhan mbeag*); it had always been an
independant kingdom and 'never lay under foreign
dominion' (*níor luidh Éire riamh faoi chumhachtaibh coigcríche*)
until the twelfth century (FFÉ i: 16, 38, 82). These two
historiographical texts provide a new and appropriate

origin legend for the emergent Catholic nation; both furnish in different, but complementary, modes the supreme literary realisation of the new orthodoxy in Irish political thought. Central to that orthodoxy was the unassailable position of the Stuarts as kings of Ireland and their unquestionable right to the crown of Ireland, a crown which, as Mageoghan had shown, existed from time immemorial.

Mageoghan's translation was not written in a vacuum, then; it obviously has to be placed in a wider context: the conscious re-writing of Irish history which was undertaken in the early decades of the seventeenth century as part of the intellectual response to the 'new political reality'. Nor was Mageoghan divorced from the literary or the political activity of the period. His kinsman, Mac Coghlan, for whom he provided his translation, was a member of the Dublin parliament and subsequently a member of the General Council of the Confederation of Kilkenny; he was also a patron of The Four Masters. Mageoghan was 'on terms of intimacy' with the principal member of that eminent group, Mícheál Ó Cléirigh, and he gave his imprimatur to certain transcriptions made by the famous scribe. He was also in touch with Ware and Usher.[20] He himself claimed that he had seen and read 'many of the principal books of Ireland':

Ataimsi Conall mac Neill Mhegeochagain o Lios Maighne a ccundae iarthair Mhidhe duine uasal ag denamh fiaghnuise go bfaca ⁊ gur léugh mé móran do phrimhleabraibh Ereann ...

(Flower 1926: 473)

There is an abundance of evidence to support his claim. According to one scribe, Mageoghan was 'one who collects and preserves the ancient monuments of our ancestors, a true bee for gathering and collecting everything that pertains to the honour and history of the Irish':

In nomine Dei Amen. An treas lá do mhí Sheptember. anno Christi. 1644. do tionnsgnadh an leabhrán so do sgríobhadh a ttígh Chonuill mhic Néill mic Rossa Mhegochagáin, etc. a Lios Maighne a cCinéill bhFiachach, aon le ttaisghitar ⁊ lé ccoimheadtar seanmhonámeintibh ar sinsar agus firbheach thiomsuighthi ⁊ thinoil gach neithe da mbeannann le honóir ⁊ le seanchus Chloinne Mhíliodh Easpáine ...

(RIA 23 D 9: 1)

Not only do *Annála Ríoghachta Éireann*, *Foras Feasa ar Éirinn* and *The Annals of Clonmacnoise* emanate from the same period, they also, obviously, emanate from the same socio-cultural and intellectual matrix. Mageoghan nowhere states overtly the contemporaneous focus of his writing, yet explicit in his narrative is the historical existence of political entities central to seventeenth-century Irish political thought: the Irish nation, the kingdom of Ireland, the crown of Ireland. These were not, according to Mageoghan and his fellow-writers, developments of early-modern Ireland; rather had they existed from time immemorial. Hobsbawm (1983), and other historians, have invoked the term 'invented tradition' to define a fairly common process whereby continuity with a suitable historic past is claimed and established for recent developments. Throughout his text Mageoghan assiduously, yet almost imperceptibly, establishes and delineates the necessary continuity. Accordingly, his earliest references to the Irish nation, the Irish kingdom and the crown of Ireland all occur in the pre-historic period:

> Nwae raigned twenty yeares and was then slaine in Moye torey ... and such of them as made escape from that danger were quite driven out of the whole kingdome twenty seven yeares after the first battaile.
>
> (A: 3v, ACl:17)

Of the comeinge of the sonns of Milesus of Spaine to this Kingdome ... How Hermion slew Heber and raigned himselfe as sole monarch of the Kingdome.

(A: 5r, AC: 21)

When any one was borne to whom to be Kinge of Ireland was predestinated ... the stone would give such a shootinge noise that it was heard from sea to sea, throughout the whole Kingdome ... This stone remained a longe time in the Kinge of Irelands palace of Taragh whereon manye kings and Queenes were crowned.

(A: 6v, AC: 26)

Soone after this conquest made by the sonnes of Milesus their kinsmen and friends, they divided the whole kingdome among themselves.

(A: 7r, AC: 27)

Ollow Fodla of the house of Ulster was kinge of Ireland ... ever after his house stocke and familie were by them in their rimes and poemes preferred before any others of their equalls of the Irish nation ...

(A: 8v, AC: 34)

Kinge Siorna went to meet them ... with all the forces of the Kingdome ... that almost both sides perished therein ... and especially the Irish nation with their kinge.

(A: 9r, AC: 36)

When Kinge Twahall was thus established in the quite possession of the Crowne and Kingome and had brought the whole Kingdome into his subjection.

(A: 14r, AC: 52)

The existence of an ancient Irish Catholic nation was a vital component of Counter-Reformation rhetoric in Ireland. The existence of the kingdom of Ireland, separate from the kingdom of England, was a central argument of Irish Catholic leaders in their attempts to come to an equitable constitutional arrangement with the Stuarts in the first half of the seventeenth century. The settlement envisaged was one that would combine continued allegiance to the King – as king of Ireland – with guarantees of civil and religious rights for his Catholic subjects. Their hopes of coming to an understanding with the King concerning the re-shaping of the government of Ireland in a manner more satisfactory to themselves was never achieved, but the contemporaneous documentation provides ample testimony to their efforts.[21] In a 'Remonstrance of Grievances' presented to the King's commissioners in March 1643 'in the behalf of the Catholics of Ireland' it is argued that

> your Majestie's kingdome of Ireland in all successions of ages, since the raigne of King Henry the Second, sometimes King of England and Lord of Ireland, had parlyaments of their own, composed of Lords and commons, in the same manner and forme, qualified with equall liberties, powers, privileges and immunities with the Parlyament of England, and onely dependant of the King and Crowne of England and Ireland.
>
> (Gilbert 1882 ii: 238)

As Beckett (1959: 35) commented, 'this may be bad history and doubtful law, but it is a fair indication of the attitudes of the men who wrote it towards the character and rights of the Irish nation.' In an anonymous tract drawn up in 1644 it is declared that

> Ireland is governed by laws and customs separate and divers from the laws of England; which proveth that it is a distinct dominion, separate from the Kingdom of England … And now, forasmuch as it cannot be denied, that Ireland is a kingdom distinct of itself …
>
> (Harris 1750 ii: 3, 21)

The demands of the 'Roman Catholics of Ireland' drawn up in 1644 included

> That an Act be passed in the next Parliament declaratory that the Parliament of Ireland is a free parliament of itself, independent of, and not subordinate to, the parliament of England, and that the subjects of Ireland are immediately subjects to your majesty as right of your Crowne.
>
> (Gilbert 1885 iii: 286)

Central to these arguments was the conviction that the king's authority in Ireland was independent of his authority in England; that Ireland was a separate kingdom, that the Irish were immediately subject to the King 'as in right of your crown' (Gilbert 1885 iii: 133). The crown of Ireland symbolized that separate kingdom and gave it a concrete iconographic existence. One of the earliest illustrations of that crown appears in an atlas compiled by Diego Homem in 1558 (BL Add. 5415A: ff 9v–10). The atlas consists of large charts on vellum with the symbols and arms of the respective sovereigns emblazoned on the various countries. Symbolizing Ireland, and accompanying its map, is a harp beneath a crown. The same 'crowned harp' appears on coins, charters, and other atlases throughout the second half of the sixteenth century (Hayes-McCoy 1979: 22–3). The crown, however, is not the closed imperial crown which accompanies the map of England, but a spiked open radiated crown depicting the distinctive crown of Ireland.

Fig. 6: Map and emblem of Ireland in Diego Homem's atlas (1558)

The same distinctive crown is worn by Brian Bóramha in a portrait of him in the first published translation of *Foras Feasa ar Éirinn* (O'Connor 1723): a crown consisting of a circlet and five visible pointed rays. The same crown was utilized by the Volunteers at the end of the eighteenth century and by O'Connell and his followers in the Repeal Association. Hayes-McCoy (1979: 89) has suggested that the 'Irish crown' found favour with the Volunteers as an ensign of sovereignty 'for the reason that, not being the imperial crown of Britain, it laid emphasis on the contemporary patriotic contention that Ireland was a distinct kingdom'. The Loyal National Appeal Association of 1840 restored the 'Irish crown' as the ensign proper to the Irish harp and it appeared as such on banners, membership cards, and other documents of the Repeal Association. And at the monster repeal meeting at Mullaghmast, Co. Kildare, in 1843 O'Connell received the 'Repeal cap' from a deputation and promised to wear it for the rest of his life.

Fig. 7: O'Connell's 'Repeal Cap'

Although in essence nothing more than a velvet green cap, it was perceived, by friend and foe alike, to be based on 'the old Milesian crown' and to represent the crown of Ireland:

> Mr O'Connell wore a cap, and I remember hearing it said, but it was not generally believed that he meant to be crowned with it at Tara.
>
> (*Report*: 614)

> A circumstance in the day's proceedings which was afterwards greatly misconstrued must be noticed. A national cap, shaped like the old 'Milesian Crown'[22] was presented to O'Connell by a deputation headed by John Hogan, the sculptor ... To the eyes of unfriendly critics it was the Irish crown which was presented and accepted ...
>
> (Duffy 1896 i: 170)

> O'Connell appeared on the platform in his crimson robes as an alderman of Dublin, and in the presence of 400,000 people, John Hogan, the sculptor ... solemnly placed on the head of the Liberator a cap of green velvet, with gold edging, in the form of the old Milesian crown. 'My only regret sir,' said Hogan, 'is that this is not of gold'. The incident seems now to savour of the stage, but at the time it was regarded as a solemn act of homage to O'Connell – the offering by the people of a crown to their Liberator.
>
> (MacDonagh 1903: 326)

According to the poets, however, it was not a cap that O'Connell was destined to wear but 'an chróin', even when fulfilling the ancient rite of sacral marriage:

> Beidh na Laighnigh go dána ag trascairt an tsló,
> is ní raghaidh as an láthair aon tSacsanach beo,
> le cúnamh na Muimhneach bheidh i dtosach an ghleo,
> beidh an chróin ar Dhónall go hórga is go meidhreach
> is luíodh lena stórach, sí Síle Ní Ghadhra.

The Leinstermen will boldly vanquish the tribe,
and not one Englishman will escape alive,
with the help of the Munstermen who will lead the fight,
the Crown will be on Dónall golden and blithely,
and let him lie with his sweetheart, Síle Ní Ghadhra.[23]

From the end of the sixteenth century to the nineteenth, the 'crown of Ireland' reverberates through Irish political rhetoric. It was, undoubtedly, one of three crowns, but one which was solely in the gift of the Irish to bestow on him they deemed to be their rightful king. It was, accordingly, granted by the native intelligentsia to the Stuarts and O'Connell; it was withheld from the usurpers William of Orange and the Georges. The 'crown of Ireland" was never deemed to be a subordinate or a subsidiary member of a unitary crown; it had its own separate existence and function: a symbol of legitimacy, of a separate kingdom, of independent authority. It is ironic, of course, that it was Henry VIII's act of 1541 which generated that seminal icon but, as argued originally by Brendan Bradshaw (1979: 267), one of the unforeseen effects of that act was that it provided 'a constitutional principle on which to base an ideology of Irish nationalism'.

Fig. 8: Cover of *O'Connell Centenary Record 1875*

1 ARÉ provides a good example of this progression.

2 See Momigliano (1950, 1958), Pocock (1957, 1961), Klempt (1960), Fussner (1962), Huppert (1968), Kelley (1970, 1998), Guenée (1973, 1980), Dubois (1977), Gilbert (1984), Woolf (1990), Helgerson (1992).

3 See Ó Buachalla (1983, 1987, 1993), Bradshaw (1993), Cunningham (2000), Carroll (2001), Dunne (2001).

4 See Murphy (1896), O'Grady (1926: 17), Flower (1926: 471), Walsh (1938), Sanderlin (1982).

5 This and the other excerpts quoted in the article are taken from the earliest manuscript copy (A) in Armagh Public Library; I also give the corresponding reference to the published edition (AC). I would like to thank the Assistant Keeper of Armagh Public Library (Ms Carol Conlin) and her staff for facilitating my research.

6 The Four Masters cite *Leabhar Cluana mic Nóis* (ARÉ i: lxiv) as one of their sources and although O'Donovan identified that text as AC, it seems that the text in question is not AC, but *Chronicum Scotorum* (Ó Muraíle 1996: 101). A copy of that text, allegedly written by Mícheál (mac Peadair) Ó Longáin (*c.* 1693–1770) in 1611 is entitled *Análadh Chluain mhic Nóis nó Cronicum Scotorum* (Ní Úrdail 2000: 37, 135). It would seem, however, that the MS in question is a nineteenth-century forgery (Ó Muraíle 1996: 309, Ó Macháin 2002: 234). O'Curry (1861: 131) believed 'that the original book was preserved in the possession of the family of the late Sir Richard Nagle, who was descended from the translator by the mother's side; however on the death of the worthy baronet, a few years ago, no trace of it could be found among the family papers'. Paul Walsh (1938: 42), thought that Mageoghan's translation 'may have been prompted by Usher ... I imagine Mageoghan assisted Usher with translations'. In a copy of a MS written by Sir James Ware in 1638/9 (Dublin Public Library, MS 169: 248) he notes 'the Annals of Clonmacnoise with Conell McGeoghegan'.

7 See Gleeson (1959: 140), Binchy (1961: 66), Radner (1978: xv), Grabowski (1984: 6), Dumville (1999: 104–5).

8 In quoting from this and subsequent poems I have normalised the orthography and supplied my own translations. For Mac Coisi, see O'Leary (1999).

9 See also Hore (1857), Hayes-McCoy (1970), Byrne (1973), Dillon (1973), Mac Cana (1973), Simms (1987: 21–40), Fitzpatrick (2004).

10 See Garstin (1903: 5–10), McClintock (1950: plates 16, 48), Hayes-McCoy (1979: 132–3), *Dictionary of the Irish language* (Royal Irish Academy, Dublin, 1983), s.v. *barr, cathbarr, corann, imscing, mind*. In *Acallamh na Senórach*, a late Middle Irish text (*Irische Texte* 4 i, 1900, p. 135, l. 4944; p. 315, n. 4942) it is related that there was a golden diadem (*mind óir*) over the head of Dairend as a sign of a queen/queenship (*i comartha rigna/a comartha righnachta*). In the twelfth-century propagandist text *Caithréim Chellacháin Chaisil*, it is related (Bugge 1905 § 7, 4, 61) that when Cellachán's followers proclaimed him king they placed 'the royal diadem round his head (*roghabhsat a mhind um a chenn)'*. This, however, may be based on some foreign model. See also Ó Corráin (1974: 69), Flanagan (1989: 202). Hayes (1949: 134) records that the Kavanagh family 'clung to and preserved the ancient gold crown of their ancestors, the Kings of Leinster. The relic … was last seen at an exhibition or museum in Toulouse shortly before the French Revolution' (I am grateful to Prof. Kevin Whelan for this reference). For the 'Comerford crown', see below n. 22.

11 Curtis (1943: 78); see also Bradshaw (1979), Moody (1976: 46–8), CSPD Henry VIII, ii, p. 480; iii, pp 304–5.

12 I have quoted from the original manuscript (Carew MSS, vol. 600, f. 190). I am most grateful to Dr Brendan Kane for drawing my attention to this passage and providing me with a copy of the original.

13 Moody (1976: 72, 85, 90–91,104–5, 121–2); Lyons (2003: 20, 88, 92).

14 The epithet, as edited, is *triath coróna* but the form in the MSS (all copies) is, as given by me, *triath corónta*. For a similar form, by the same poet, see above p. 31. Greene did not discuss the problem, but it is obvious that he substituted *coróna* for metrical reasons (*corónta* does not provide a full rime with *onóra*). There is no reason to assume however that poets – even bardic poets – sought or achieved 100% perfection every day; they also must have nodded from time to time. The only other form of the word which would provide full rime with *onóra* is *corónna* < *corónda* an attested variant of *corónta*.

15 'Coróin Éireann ainm Uí Néill' (Ó Gnímh), source: Book of O' Conor Don: 135b.

16 Cf. 'K. Moyleseachlin … K. of all Ireland, having thus triumphantly raigned over all Ireland … this was the last Kinge of Ireland of Irish blood that had Crowne. Yett there were seaven kings after without Crowne befor the cominge of the English …

Herafter followeth a discourse of the 7 Kinges of Ireland that lived without a Crowne' (A: 49r–50r, AC: 171).

17 Gwynn's (1953: 197) statement that 'Mageoghan's picturesque translation of the lost Annals of Clonmacnoise preserves what seems to be the earliest version of the legend' is obviously not true. O'Mahony (1857: 591) alludes to the story but adds 'it is evident from all the records of his time, that he [Donnchadh] had never become possessed of any crown or regalia of Ireland, which he could so bestow'. In the late 1640s it was widely rumoured that the Pope intended sending 'the crown' to the Ulster leader Owen Rua O Neill. See, Aiazza (1873: 385), Casway (1984: 208–9), Kavanagh (1932: 60).

18 Silke (1955), Ó Buachalla (1993, 1996: 24–5).

19 Ó Muraíle (2002: 113) points out that the title of the printed edition (*Annála Ríoghachta Éireann*) does not occur in the body of the text. This is technically correct, but it is obvious that it is based on the title *Annales regni Hiberniae* used in the contemporary approbations accompanying the text (ARÉ i: lxx). It is not irrevelant to point out that Ó Muraíle's comment is contained in an article and a book incorporating the title *Beatha Aodha Ruaidh* – a title which is nowhere to be found in the text in question.

20 Walsh (1918: 9, 1938: 43), Flower (1926: 473), Cox (1973), Sanderlin (1982: 121), Nicholls (1983), Ó Siochrú (1999: 37, 265), Cunningham (2000: 77), Ní Mhurchú & Breatnach (2001: 64, 81).

21 See Clarke (1990, 2000); Ó Buachalla (1993).

22 It was believed, it seems, that the cap was based on 'the Comerford crown' which, according to O'Connor (1723: iii–iv) was discovered in a bog in Co. Tipperary in 1692. O'Connor represents this 'provincial crown' in the lower left corner of his portrait of Brian Bóramha (above p. 33) and elsewhere in his book (p. iv). It is also incorporated into the crown depicted in the *O'Connell Centenary Record* (Fig. 8, p. 48).

23 From a poem (*Ní rugadh in Éirinn le réimis na ríoraí*) in MS RIA 23 I 48: 169.

BIBLIOGRAPHY

Abbreviations

A   The earliest copy of the text (1660) in The Public
          Library, Armagh
AC   The text as edited by Murphy (1896)
ARÉ   *Annála Ríoghachta Éireann* i-vii (ed. J. O'Donovan,
          1856, Dublin)
BL   British Library
CSPD   *Calendar of state papers, domestic* (1856–1972,
          London)
CSPI   *Calendar of state papers of Ireland* (1860–1910.
          London)
FFÉ   *Foras Feasa ar Éirinn* i–iv (ed. D. Comyn & P.
          Dinneen, ITS 4, 8, 9, 15, 1902–14. Dublin)
HMC   Historical Manuscripts Commission
ITS   Irish Texts Society
LL   *The Book of Leinster* i (ed. R.I. Best, O. Bergin &
          M.A. O'Brien, Dublin, 1954)
RC   *Revue Celtique* (Paris 1870–)
RIA   Royal Irish Academy
TCD   Trinity College, Dublin

Aiazza, J. 1873. *The embassy in Ireland*. Dublin.

Beckett, J. C. 1959. 'The Confederation of Kilkenny Revisited', *Historical Studies* ii: 29–41.

Bergin, O. J. 1921. 'A Dialogue Between Donnchadh Son of Brian and Mac Coise', *Ériu* 9: 175–80.

Binchy, D. A. 1921. 'An Irish Ambassador at the Spanish Court', *Studies* 10: 357–73, 573–84.

1961. 'Lawyers and Chroniclers' in *Seven centuries of Irish learning* (ed. B. Ó Cuív), 58–71.

Bouchart, A. 1520. *Les grandes croniques de Bretagne* (ed. G. Jeanneau, Paris, 1971).

Bradshaw, B. 1979. *The Irish constitutional revolution of the sixteenth century*. Cambridge.

1993. 'Geoffrey Keating: Apologist of Irish Ireland' in *Representing Ireland* (ed. B. Bradshaw, Cambridge, 1993), 166–190.

Breatnach, P. A. (ed.) 1973. 'Marbhna Aodha Ruaidh Uí Dhomhnaill', *Éigse* 15: 31–50.

Brewer, J. S. & Buyllen, W. (eds) 1870. *Calendar of the Carew Manuscripts 1601–1603*. London.

Bugge, A. 1905. *Caithreim Ceallachain Caisil*. Christiana.

Byrne, F. J. 1973. *Irish kings and high-kings*. London.

Carroll, C. 2001. *Circe's cup*. Cork.

Casway, J. I. 1984. *Owen Roe O'Neill and the struggle for catholic Ireland*. Philadelphia.

Clarke, A. 1990. 'Colonial Constitutional Attitudes in Ireland, 1640–60', *Proceedings of the Royal Irish Academy* 90 C: 357–75.

2000. 'Patrick Darcy And the Constitutional Relationship Between Ireland and Britain' in *Political thought in seventeenth-century Ireland*. (ed. J. H. Ohlmeyer, Cambridge, 2000), 35–55.

Cox, L. 1973. 'The Mac Coghlans of Delvin Eachtra', *Irish Genealogist* 4: 534–46.

Cunningham, B. 2000. *The world of Geoffrey Keating*. Dublin.

Curtis, E. 1941. 'The O'Maolchonaire Family', *Galway Archaeological and Historical Society* 19: 118–46.

& McDowell, R. B. (eds) 1943. *Irish historical documents 1172–1922*. London.

de Mariana, J. 1601. *Historia general de España*. Toledo.

Dillon, M. 1973. 'The Inauguration of Irish Kings', *Celtica* 10: 1–8.

Dinneen, P. S. & O'Donoghue, T. 1911. *Dánta Aodhagáin Uí Rathaille* (ITS iii). London.

Dubois, G. 1977. *La conception de l'histoire en France, 1560–1610*. Paris.

Duffy, C. Gavan. 1896. *Young Ireland i–ii*. London.

Du Haillon, Bernard de Girard. 1571. *Histoire de France*. Paris

Dumville, D. 1999. 'A Millennium of Gaelic Chronicling', in *The medieval chronicle* (ed. E. Kooper, Amsterdam), 104–5.

Dunne, T. 2001. 'Worlds We Have Lost', *Irish Review* 27: 207–11.

Fitzpatrick, E. 2004. *Royal inauguration in Gaelic Ireland, c. 1100–1600.* Woodbridge.

Flanagan, M.T. 1989. *Irish society, Anglo-Norman settlers, Angevian kingship.* Oxford.

Flower, R. 1926. *Catalogue of Irish manuscripts in the British Museum.* vol.ii. London.

Foster, R.F. 1988. *Modern Ireland 1600–1972.* London.

Fussner, F. S. 1962. *The historical revolution: English historical writing and thought, 1580–1640.* London.

Garstin, J. R. 1903. 'President's Address', *Journal of the Royal Society of Antiquaries of Ireland* 33: 1–24.

Gilbert, F. 1984. *Machiaveli and Guicciardini: politics and history in sixteenth-century Florence.* Princeton.

Gilbert, J. T. (ed.) 1882–91. *History of the Irish confederation and the war in Ireland 1641–1643.* i–vii. Dublin.

Gilles, N. 1566. *Les chroniques et annales de France.* Paris.

Gleeson, D. & Mac Airt, S. 1959. 'The Annals of Roscrea', *Proceedings of the Royal Irish Academy* 59 C: 137– 80.

Grabowski, K. & Dumville, D. 1984. *Chronicles and annals of medieval Ireland & Wales.* Woodbridge.

Greene, D. 1972. *Duanaire Mhéig Uidhir.* Dublin.

Guenée, B. 1973. 'Histoire, Annales, Chroniques', *Annales* 28: 997–1016.
    1980. *Histoire et culture historique dans l'occident medieval.* Paris.

Guicciardini, F. 1621. *La historia d'Italia.* Geneva.

Gwynn, A. 1953. 'Ireland and the Continent in the Eleventh Century', *Irish Historical Studies* 8: 193–216.

Harris, W. 1750. *Hibernica.* Dublin.

Hayes, R. 1949. *Biographical dictionary of Irishmen in France.* Dublin.

Hayes-McCoy, G. A. 1970. 'The Making of an O'Neill', *Ulster Journal of Archaeology* 33: 89–94.
    1979. *A history of Irish flags from earliest times.* Dublin.

Helgerson, R. 1992. *Forms of nationhood: The Elizabethan writing of England.* Chicago.

Hennessy, W. H.1866. *Chronicum Scotorum.* London.

Hobsbawm, E. & Ranger, T. 1983. *The invention of tradition.* Cambridge.

Hore, H. F. 1857. 'Inauguration of Irish Chiefs', *Ulster Journal of Archaeology* 5: 216–35.

Huppert, G. 1968. 'Naissance de l'Histoire en France' *Annales* 23: 69–105.

Kavanagh, S. (ed.), 1932. *Commentarius Rinuccianus.* vol. iii. Dublin.

Kelley, D. R. 1970. *The foundations of modern historical scholarship.* New York.

1998. *Faces of history: historical inquiry from Herodotus to Herder.* New Haven.

Klempt, A. 1960. *Die Säkularisierung der universalhistorischen Auffassung zum Wandel des Geschichtsdenkens im 16 und 17. Jahrhundert.* Göttingen.

La Popelinière, Henry Voisin de, 1599. *Dessein de l'histoire nouvelle des François.* Paris.

Lynch, J. 1662. *Cambrensis eversus.* St. Malo. (ed. M. Kelly, Dublin, 1848).

Lyons, M. A. 2003. *Franco-Irish relations, 1500–1610.* London.

Mac Airt, S. & Mac Niocaill, G. (eds) 1983. *The annals of Ulster.* Dublin.

Mac Cana, P. 1973. 'The *Topos* of the Single Sandal in Irish Tradition', *Celtica* 10: 160–66.

Mac Curtin, H. 1717. *A brief discourse in vindication of the antiquity of Ireland.* Dublin.

Mhág Craith. C. (ed.) 1967. *Dán na mbráthar mionúr.* Dublin.

McClintock, H. F. 1950. *Old Irish and Highland dress.* Dundalk.

MacDonagh, M. 1903. *The life of Daniel O'Connell.* London.

McKenna, L. (ed.), 1918. *Iomarbhágh na bhfileadh.* London.

1939. *Aithdhioghluim dána.* Dublin.

Meyer, K. 1907. 'A Medley of Irish Texts', *Archiv für Celtische Lexicogrophie* 3 iv: 302–26.

Moody, T. W. (*et al.*), 1976. *A new history of Ireland.* iii. Oxford.

Momigliano, A. D. 1950. 'Ancient History and the Antiquarian', *Journal of the Warburg and Courtauld Institutes* 13: 285–315.

1958. *Histoire et historiens dans l'antiquité.* Geneva.

Murphy, D. (ed.), 1896. *The annals of Clonmacnoise.* Dublin.

Nicholls, K. 1983. 'The Mac Coghlans', *Irish Genealogist* 6: 445–60.

Ní Mhurchú, M. & Breatnach, D. 2001. *Beathaisnéis 1560–1781.* Dublin.

Ní Úrdail, M. 2000. *The scribe in eighteenth- and nineteenth-century Ireland.* Münster.

Ó Buachalla, B. 1983. '*Annála Ríoghachta Éireann* is *Foras Feasa ar Éirinn*: An Comhthéacs Comhaimseartha', *Studia Hibernica* 22/3: 59–105.

1987. Foreword to reprint of FFÉ.

1993. '*James Our True King* : The Ideology of Irish Royalism in the Seventeenth Century' in *Political thought in Ireland since the seventeenth century* (ed. D. G. Boyce *et al.*, London, 1993), 1–35.

1996. *Aisling ghéar.* Dublin.

Ó Corráin. D. 1974. 'Caithréim Chellacháin Chaisil: History or Propaganda', *Ériu* 25: 1–69.

O'Connor, D. 1723. *The general history of Ireland.* Dublin.

O'Curry, E. 1861. *Lectures on the manuscript materials of ancient Irish history.* Dublin.

O'Donovan, J. 1861. *Leabhar na g-Ceart.* Dublin.

O Flaherty, R. 1685. *Ogygia.* London (trans. J.Hely, Dublin, 1793).

O'Grady, S. H. 1926. *Catalogue of Irish manuscripts in the British Museum.* vol. i. London.

O'Leary, A. 1999. 'The Identities of the Poet(s) Mac Coisi: A Reinvestigation', *Cambrian Medieval Celtic Studies* 38: 53–72.

Ó Macháin, P. 2002. Review of Ní Úrdail (2000), *Éigse* 33:233–7.

O'Mahony, J. 1857. *The history of Ireland*. New York.

Ó Muraíle, N. 1996. *The celebrated antiquary Dubhaltach Mac Fhirbhisigh*. Maynooth.

    2002. 'Paul Walsh as Editor and Explicator of *Beatha Aodha Ruaidh'* in Ó Riain (ed.), 98–123.

O'Rahilly, C. (ed.) 1952. *Five seventeenth-century political poems*. Dublin.

Ó Riain, P. (ed.) 2002. *Beatha Aodha Ruaidh* (ITS Subsidiary Series 12). Dublin.

Ó Siochrú, M. 1999. *Confederate Ireland 1642–1649*. Dublin.

Pocock, G. J. A. 1957. *The ancient constitution and the feudal law*. Cambridge.

    1961. 'The Origins of the Study of the Past: A Comparative Approach', *Comparative Studies in Society and History* 4: 209–46.

Radner, J. 1978. *Fragmentary annals of Ireland*. Dublin.

Ranum, O. 1975. *National consciousness: history and political culture in early modern Europe*. Baltimore.

Report of the trial of William Smith O'Brien. 1849. Dublin.

Sanderlin, S. 1982. 'The Manuscripts of The Annals of Clonmacnois', *Proceedings of the Royal Irish Academy*, 82 C: 11– 23.

Silke, J. J. 1955.'Primate Lombard and James I', *Irish Theological Quarterly* 22: 134–50.

    1966. *Ireland and Europe*. Dundalk.

Simms, K. 1987. *From kings to warlords*. Woodbridge.

Stokes, W. 1895–7. 'The Annals of Tigernach', *Revue Celtique* 16–8.

Stow, J. 1631. *The annals of England*. London.

Van Caenegem, R. C. (ed.) 1978. *Guide to sources of medieval history*. Amsterdam.

Walsh, P. 1918. *Genealogiae regum et sanctorum Hiberniae*. Dublin.

    1932. 'Notes on Two Mageoghegans' *Irish Book Lover* 20: 75–81.

    1938. *The Mageoghans*. Mullingar.

Woolf, D. R. 1990. *The idea of history in early Stuart England*. Toronto.